Rumination
About
the Fruit of the Spirit

Patience

*A funny thing happened on the way
to quitting smoking*

I got a life

By
April Heather

Author April Heather
Edited by Dar Streedbeck
Printed by CreateSpace
Made in the United States of America
ISBN-13: 978-1494304164
ISBN-10: 1494304163

Be on the lookout for these other titles by April Heather

Winter of 2013-2014
        Rumination About the Fruit of the Spirit: Kindness
        Rumination About the Fruit of the Spirit: Goodness
        Rumination About the Fruit of the Spirit: Gentleness
        Rumination About the Fruit of the Spirit: Faithfulness
        Rumination About the Fruit of the Spirit: Self-control

Rumination about the fruit of the spirit: Patience

"But the fruit of the spirit is

love, joy, peace,

patience, kindness, goodness,

faithfulness, gentleness & self-control.

Against such things there is no law."

Galatians 5:22, 23 NIV

"Let us not become conceited, provoking and

envying each other."

Galatians 5:26 NIV

Prologue

My grandmother was the best Christian in the world. It's just too bad I didn't respect the fact that she was. Back when I was between the ages of twelve and fourteen, I was too busy being mad at my warm and loving grandma for being a teacher and acting like one. Especially since she was retired from the local school district and **especially since** we weren't in school. We were at her kitchen table, at my favorite place in the whole world, my grandparent's farm in southeastern South Dakota; and she was wrecking it by being a teacher. When it came to school, any type of school, there was no rest for that woman. She was always dragging my younger sisters and me off to Sunday School, Vacation Bible School, church and then she would assign us homework with study books in math and English that she chose from the magazine rack in the grocery store.

In this particular instance, she was making us memorize Bible verses every day. My way of thinking was that it was summer and I could get that kind of grief at home during the school year. Why couldn't she just be a grandma? Well, she **was** being a grandma. **My** grandma. I suppose she was struggling too, because if she was a teacher, then why wasn't I a better student? Even more annoying, the two younger girls were rattling off their memorized pieces so well. Boy, did I get mad at that. When it came to this "fruit of the spirit" verse, I was fed up with the process and had had enough; I let her know it. It was probably the only time I ever won an argument with her. I knew it, too. It caught me off guard and I was surprised there wasn't more pleasure in winning. Even though it was no fun and games, the pressure was off and with that came relief.

Cut to fifteen years later; I was married with two children and I recognized this Bible verse immediately while I was driving home and saw it on a banner hanging from a church. I remember it being up there longer than any other banner that has ever been posted in this town, and it was there for me to ponder every day as I drove by. Since I didn't have to memorize the thing, I could now see the wisdom in it. When I got home, I showed my kids its location in Galatians and then wrote it down in the back of their Bibles. We discussed it a little bit and every once in while we will make a reference to "use your virtues" or "use your fruits." I DID NOT make them memorize it.

Well, just about another ten years after that, I was nearly 40 and a funny thing happened on the way to quitting smoking. It was Christmas time and as usual, I was preparing myself to quit smoking and eventually fail again for the new year. Everywhere I looked I saw LOVE, JOY, and PEACE and I remember thinking, "Where is the rest of it?" You know...the rest of the verse, because Grandma placed such a huge importance on memorizing the whole thing, not just the first three words. Then I got to thinking that everybody is constantly on the search for happiness and yet all the promotion stops after love, joy, and peace. That is when it occurred to me that maybe you can't get to the love, joy, and peace unless you first enact the patience, kindness, goodness, faithfulness, gentleness, and self-control.

Invigorated by my new epiphany, I made the decision to spend the next day looking for any and all ways to extend patience. It was a passive day, spent watching and learning, more than it was about controlling and doing. That night, I had gained so much information that I decided to do it again the very next day. The third and fourth day, I took a break to be normal for a couple of days. I didn't want to hold myself accountable for not meeting new standards of behavior. That seemed exhausting. I was looking for love, joy, and peace. I was looking for freedom. I was looking for a way to stabilize my life so I could allow the process of withdrawal to happen when I quit smoking. During the third and fourth days, I tried to go about my day normally while weighing my new information against life's usual routine. A couple days later, I did the practice all over again, except I moved on to the virtue of kindness. I kept at it until I had made it through the remaining six fruits of the verse.

From the get-go I had mini-explosions of epiphany after epiphany. I decided to postpone my New Year's quit date and I kept on going with the next virtue. Most of this was about watching and learning; at this time I wasn't after any permanent changes to my attitude or routine. I got curious ... then tested it to see what would happen. I did do a round two with the intent to apply some changes and I found it didn't require an overhaul of my life. It mostly was the result of, *"If you know better you do better."* (Maya Angelou)

Talk about a slow learner! I had thought I was having trouble learning the verse sitting at the kitchen table with my grandma and look what I just admitted to you. Learning a lesson after what -- twenty-five years maybe? You know, I had never really wanted to re-live my childhood, nor do I want a do-over. But man, if I could have applied this to my twenties right before I became a parent ... that would have been ... Wow! ... to have learned how to handle stress instead of avoiding it. ... To have been seated comfortably inside my own character ... at rest in my parental resolve. It would have been career changing ... life changing! At least I *think* all these things, because I am feeling pretty good right now. Some of this good feeling could have come with age but still ... I could've and should've known then what I know now ... because I knew this verse back then. Now, the best I can do is pass my lessons on to others like me and to the next generation.

Maybe I oversimplify when I boil **all** the answers into one single Bible verse, because there is more to reducing stress and living a balanced lifestyle, but this verse sums it up pretty well. *(Gal. 5:22, 23 NIV)* "But the fruit of the spirit is love, joy, peace, patience, kindness, goodness, faithfulness, gentleness, and self-control. Against such things there is no law." Soon after it, verse 26 says, "Let us not become conceited, provoking, and envying each other." As I put each virtue into daily practice, I came to view the Fruits of the Spirit as the "do's" and most of the Ten Commandments as the "don'ts."

Just take a moment to think this over ... if you concentrate on these virtues, you don't have to worry about breaking the law because **against such things there are no laws.** In today's over-regulated world, there might be a few regulations to enforce the positive; but for the most part, our laws are a preventive maintenance tool to control the negative.

Now to be sure, I am not talking about crisis mode. I am talking about everyday living, and life darting from moment to moment. You know at some point in the next few hours that someone or something is going to clamor for your attention. The moment is yours to respond: are you going to choose a fruit to apply it to the distraction, or are you going to get exasperated at the source?

In keeping with my epiphany that "you need to enact the rest of the verse to achieve the love, joy, and peace," I wrote my experiences with Patience in one book, Kindness in another book, and a book each for Goodness, Faithfulness, Gentleness, and Self-control. Six books in all.

They don't have to be read in any particular order. For that reason this prologue accompanies all of them and you only need to read this once. In the next book, you can get started right away with Chapter One.

With that, we will pick the fruit of the day. Let's see ... which one did you choose?

Patience

Patience: noun
The capacity to accept or tolerate delay, trouble, or suffering without getting angry or upset

-2010 New Oxford American Dictionary 3rd edition

Patience: noun
1 (ex.: she tried everyone's patience) forbearance, tolerance, restraint, self-restraint, stoicism, calmness, composure, equanimity, imperturbability, phlegm, understanding, indulgence.

2 (ex.: a task requiring patience) perseverance, persistence, endurance, tenacity, assiduity, application, staying power, doggedness, determination, resolve, resolution, resoluteness.

-2008 Oxford American Writer's Thesaurus 2nd edition

Chapter 1   Patience

Phlegm? *(from the thesaurus entry on the last page)* Phlegm?! I have no idea why "phlegm" is listed in the Oxford American Writers Thesaurus as another word for "patience." Using patience does help me to clear my mind and find out if I have all the facts before I start thinking, but patience is the tool; it is not the stuff I am clearing away. Man, the things you learn when looking up words you thought you knew. Phlegm? No wonder we are disgusted with patience and get irrational as we plunge on.

Over and over again, long before this project, I found there is a huge difference between what I *think* is going on and what is *really* going on. It starts off so innocently, then the two clash because my brain refuses to submit and accept what is real. Next, my ego arrives to take its last stand against reality, then suddenly disappears while leaving embarrassed people in its wake and I'm left with a new lesson in what is real. Each discovery into the unknown begins with the patience to accept something new. If I could accept what is being presented in the first place, without a fight, I could probably save myself some time and some embarrassment.

I went into this foray with my fruity epiphany, knowing full well there would be occasions when I wouldn't *want* to be patient. For example, I wanted to think ahead, I wanted to continue covering my bases, and I wanted to practice preventive maintenance. The best time saver is to "stop it before it starts," right? Wrong. Doing thirty things unnecessarily to cover all the potential possibilities is a major time waster. And there were times I didn't **want** to use patience -- I was mad and just wanted to be difficult; or, when I thought I would receive an outcome I didn't want. I learned that I had to use patience even when I felt like I was letting my guard down. This took some restraint and practice, because I had to fight off the feeling of being unprotected and exposed. I especially didn't want to be the idiot that should have seen it coming.

In general, we think patience needs to be exercised when the pace is slow, which makes sense. You will hear most people claim to lose their patience during the mundane practices of life. For instance, you need to tap into patience when you really need to get on to the next stage of your day and you are stuck at the store while the checkout line is hardly moving; when you are on hold for the next customer service representative; or with people who are slow to get the concept: that's the easy part. I know when you are in your struggle with patience it doesn't **seem** easy, but it's what we practice when things are slow so it becomes what we all know.

The hard part is to extend patience when things are going fast! rapid! quick! We need to use patience when we are on the edge of getting snappy, because we think we are short on time. In a world where everybody is in a hurry, we believe there is no time for patience.

I'm trying to explain that my great discovery, right before quitting smoking was … that using patience during these periods won't slow you down. In fact it will probably speed things up, because sentences are completed without interruption. Concepts are fully visualized before motion is wasted. Using patience helps to keep your brain clear and your hearing open to what is **actually** being said, instead of getting sidetracked with what you **think** someone is saying ... which leads to doing the wrong thing ... then stumbling onto what is really going on ... to finally realizing what WAS actually said earlier ... and bumbling through an explanation because you didn't have the patience to listen five minutes ago. Then you get all amped up, bent out of shape and stomp off to smoke so you can unscramble your brains and cool down.

See what I mean with the bumbling explanations? They take up time and get in the way of the real conversation.

I used to be a busybody. I didn't know I was. I didn't want to be. I thought I was jumping in and helping. I thought I was sharing knowledge. I thought I was troubleshooting. I thought I was participating as a team member. Instead, I projected this strange mix of being dominant, getting in the way, and not trusting others to do their part. Which really doesn't sound like anything I wanted to be.

Patience becomes an excellent filter for useless actions. Especially during hectic moments. For example: I no longer answer questions that aren't mine to answer. Instead of reciting a speech starting with the wrong thing that leads to the correct thing, I just pause for a beat and say the correct thing. There is less stress, less anger, less confusion, less embarrassment, less recovery, less interruption, less invasion of a person's space.

The side effects are more trust, an increased comfort zone, a sense of being heard, a respect for others and a stronger sense of participating in a community. Most of the stuff I now contribute is relevant and because of that, I continue to participate rather than get mad and withdraw.

When I do revert to my old ways or simply make a mistake, I recover much faster because I don't need to protect my reputation and prove that it was anything other than what I had just said. I screw up; I get over it. I have to exercise patience with myself because I'm not perfect. It is just as important as exercising patience with others.

Since my little project with these virtues, I'm less tense, more efficient, and more composed in any given situation. I was horrified when I realized that my being impatient made me appear afraid; especially when I was under the delusion that I was proactive by staying on top of things. I saw enough improvement to encourage me to do the work and incorporate it into my character almost immediately. Sadly, it's not as if people noticed and complimented me on the change. Then again, I didn't want anyone to notice that I was doing the work. Eventually, respect naturally came my way as the new norm took over. Even though the new commonplace goes **undetected**, it eventually becomes the **accepted**.

Chapter 2   Stress

Oddly, I found the need to use patience even when I'm alone. Normally my day ends with twenty things left to do, only to wake up the next day and try again from the beginning. Whenever I have the chance to sit still, the fear of being lazy creeps into my solitude. My mind fills up with this constant inner chatter, trying to find a way to do those twenty things, because they are forever pushed onto tomorrow's list and I just want them done.

Then someone always comes along and adds another thing to do.

You know, I always considered myself a hopeful, positive person, so why was my default mode constantly on the verge of negativity? My routine was to end my long day of working and running errands by watching my TV shows with my feet up, then I would feel like crap for sitting there because I wasn't getting to my *list of things to do*. Most of my downtime was spent wallowing in "Why, oh why can't I get it all done?" I would get stressed out because bills were always due, the kids needed attention, I always needed to clean the house, and there was always a looming deadline. Or, whenever I had a chance to sit, I was reminded that I should be exercising instead.

It seemed I had this insidious attitude that sitting in a room by myself was proving me to be a farce; my productivity was only posturing for other people ... that I needed an audience to prove I was a worthy person who got things done. I couldn't be found sitting alone, doing nothing with my list undone. **Busted!** I would be pointed out as a fake and then held accountable for putting up false pretenses. (Or so went the delusion.)

After a while I would get tired of sitting in the negativity and I would begrudgingly get up and do what I could around the house. If it was too late to cook supper, I would go through the drive-through before the kids went to bed. Then maybe do laundry and put things away, but it wasn't like I could vacuum while everyone was asleep. Things would still go unfinished, no matter how much I got done. Since the list was just going to start all over again the next day, I would get tired and upset that I wasn't in bed, too.

You know, any advice to take a bubble bath or to get a massage to de-stress just never worked. Basically for the same reason as being idle with an unfinished list, plus, the time that was put into a massage or a bath could've been used to get my "things" done. Spending money on stress-reducing techniques like a luxury spa treatment, would add more stress, especially when bills were due. Between time and money, those techniques got me nowhere.

It took a lot of practice to sit there and know that the evil wasn't going to get me just because I was idle. I had to learn how to sit there without fretting that "time is money," or that I had to be the vigilant Warrior Mom, or getting stressed out because "a woman's work is never done." It was unproductive. To confront these head on, I would plant my butt on the couch to exemplify doing nothing and force myself to sit with convictions that everything was okay. I would actually chant in my head, "I am not naughty, naughty, naughty. I am an adult." Then I would switch the chant to "Enjoy the mundane, enjoy the mundane, enjoy the mundane." This was pretty mundane, so I had to enjoy it. Mostly at this point, if I couldn't sit there and be happy, my goal was to not get upset or stress myself out. With practice I gained some patience. Now patience comes more naturally.

Eventually I figured out nothing really changed but my attitude. Now I enjoy the down time and I don't worry about things that don't get done. This alone helps to preserve the energy for when I do get to my chores. I don't get on myself for being lazy, or whine all the way through tackling my to-do list. Since I don't mind getting started and since I'm not procrastinating, I now get to bed earlier. No longer preoccupied with my unfinished list, I am prepared to include more things in my routine, such as exercising. It took some serious convincing that my world was okay and to rest in the fact that it **will** be okay. I didn't need to go through the process of worrying until things were done. With patience I found that I didn't need to fret over things. I found that I can care without worry.

Chapter 3   Embrace Your B Side

When I quit smoking and began to write about it, I had wanted to write about my struggle with being a Type A wanna-be and my attempt to embrace a Type B lifestyle. I figured I better check into it to make sure I knew what I was talking about. To my surprise, the Type A and Type B personality labels were created in the 1950's by a couple of cardiologists to describe conditions for heart health. Type A's were labeled as hard workers who were always striving under constant stress to be the first and to be the best, and were more likely to develop coronary heart disease. As part of their health regimen these people were to take on a less stressful, Type B, lifestyle.

Wait!

Being Type A wasn't supposed to be a good thing?

Type B was supposed to be the winning lifestyle.

Say what?

I felt duped.

When I had been a teenager, a teacher of mine had handed us these sheets listing examples: "If Type A and

Type B went to the beach, Type A would be windsurfing; Type B would be reading a book. If Type A and Type B were going to get a job in business, Type A would be on Wall Street making tons of money; Type B would be employed in retail with 40-hour work weeks." Somehow, I had formed the conclusion that living as a Type B wasn't going to lead to a spectacular life. Since I was also taught that you can be anything you want to be, I had made up my mind to be a Type A. Even back then I knew I was fighting against my natural tendencies to be a Type B.

Now several years later, I learn that Type A is not a buzzword for spectacular super-humans who win at life. It was set up as a warning for us to take notice. We weren't supposed to take the personality on. The goal was for us to take measures to embrace a Type B lifestyle.

Wow! Type B's aren't lazy people! They aren't meandering souls unaffected by world causes because their heads are in the clouds. Well, befuddle me! Immediately, I wondered what kind of world would we be living in if they had switched it and labeled the moderate lifestyle as Type A. Especially since nobody wants to be labeled second place. You know, because it's natural for a student to go after the A, to compete for the blue ribbon, or just for the fact that the B side of a 45 rpm record is not the number one hit. Except for the occasional exception, of course. If those doctors had wanted a bunch of overachievers to *achieve* a more moderate lifestyle, why couldn't they have called the Type B a Type A?

I found it a fascinating read. You can do an internet search by entering "Type A Type B," and also with "Meyer Friedman," or with "Ray H. Rosenman." These heart doctors had to reupholster the chairs in their waiting room unexpectedly early. The designer pointed out that the chairs were worn through the seat and the arms but not the backs. With a little investigation and a little watching and learning, they discovered all their heart patients were pensively sitting on the edge of the seats and gripping the arm rests. These patients also wore them out in double time, because they were getting up and sitting down repeatedly to ask the receptionist, "How much longer?"

So let go of the glossy, romantic image that Type A's are untiring go-getters who live to the full extent and win. Originally that was slated for a heart attack waiting to happen ... Literally! Also, we should purge the image that Type B's meditate and meander barefoot through the world. Both types have purpose and drive, they merely go about it differently.

At some point in my mid 30s, I discovered that me running as a Type A person was just solving one panic and moving on to the next. That is when I began to let go of control and buck against the competition to be an Type A personality.

If we are to collectively move away from the "heart attack" description, we should redefine both of these dynamic personalities as clean, healthy and welcoming options for fulfilling one's life. Since there isn't a new description in place yet, I have quit being a Type A wanna-be and have embraced my B side. I find I still have my drive and get things done with excellence, just like any Type A person.

Chapter 4   Drop The Competition

One of my earliest memories centers on competition. My parents took me to a child's birthday party. I was about two or three years old and too young to know anyone. As part of the backyard celebration, they had strung up a piñata from a tree. The hosts were polite enough to let me take my turn with the bigger kids and have a whack at it. Come to think of it, that was my first experience in failure: me trying to manage a stick bigger than I was, in the direction of a swinging piñata. It was met with a crowd of polite but pitiful "ooh's" before it got serious with cheers for the older kids who were next in line.

Then I found out what success was, when someone whacked it and all this magnificent candy fell everywhere. This was quickly followed by a mad dash of everyone else knowing what was going on. Attempting to follow instructions from my parents, I toddled toward the mound of candy that had tumbled onto the ground and was knocked over by some greedy boy. Through tears of pain, I managed to spot and acquire a few outlying pieces in the grass beyond the crowd. In the end I had my pitiful handful of candy, while I watched others walk away from the debacle with mounds of candy so large that they had to lift the hems of their shirts to carry it all.

My first fully formed concept in life was "competition" and my reaction was that it sucks and it's painful. Every Easter after that, our egg hunt was faintly tainted with this piñata memory. Since my cousin and I were the oldest, we were told to give up nearly half of our candy to those younger than us who didn't find enough.

"Life is not fair."

What is the purpose of the hunt anyway? Couldn't we do this differently if all you are supposed to do is give up your winnings? My cousin and I both thought the whole thing was screwy. We decided to take on the responsibility of hiding the eggs and forego hunting them, pretty young. In both the fiesta and the Easter egg hunt, I think nearly everyone could agree that the activity is fun. It's at the end when everyone worries about being fair, that it all sours.

My parents may have a different memory of that piñata in the backyard or may have none at all. I realize this celebration didn't go the way they had planned. Their encouragement was for me to learn how to participate. The shower of candy was supposed to be fun, almost magical. In fact, that part still seems attractive. I know I would have encouraged my children to do the same, because those are the rules of the game.

From there, the push and nudge for competition just never stops. We're told that to get along in life you have to compete to find success and I hated it, because I already knew that I seldom win. Yet, competition was everywhere in everything I did and with everyone I knew. Some of my ditziest, rudest and most regrettable moments were when I was trying to find a win somewhere and went "boo-yah" when there was no "boo-yah" to be had. When I did win, I hardly got the cheers, because the competition ended with people standing around wondering what went wrong. It was so natural nobody knew they were doing it. Including me. Whenever I did get a pat on the back, it usually had come after an "oh yeah," under their breath because someone suddenly remembered their manners and then called out "Great job," to the others as a reminder to congratulate the winner. Well, maybe early on there were a couple of times when I was the only one jumping up and down shouting, "I won! I won!" probably in great disbelief. Then the coach or teacher told me to not be a sore winner, instead of telling the other kids to not be sore losers. They got me coming and going. I just couldn't win.

Conversations were even infected with competition. I'd get a few words into a sentence and people would shout witty comebacks that had nothing to do with the subject. Other times people raced me for the end of my sentence and shouted out guesses like some game show. The simplest conversations had become a huge chore as my topic gave way to test someone else's comedic venture; or, they discovered they weren't mind readers and my topic was left behind as we discussed how they came up with their topic. I just got really annoyed, as everyone vied for a chance to talk, or didn't know how to give a straight answer, so they said everything else *but* the answer.

Competition also shows up as raising the bar. For some reason when people tell me about their new "stuff," they need to litter the conversation with how much better it is than *my* "stuff." I didn't set the bar and then dared them to top it, yet, these people can't stick to talking about their stuff, they have this *need* to compare it with mine. Or, they go to the other extreme: people will compete for the sucky position, interrupting with "Think that's bad? Mine's worse ..." Even when I wasn't saying anything was bad at all. I wish I could control the world and get people to quit setting the bar and then blame others for it. Their inferiority is their problem. When people achieve their goals, they aren't thinking of you. Since I can only control myself and not others, I usually let them yammer on while I slowly lose enthusiasm for celebrating their achievement with them.

I was exhausted. I was done with finding every little opportunity to step things up and make it faster, bigger, stronger, and more luxurious. Besides, anytime I wanted to rest and enjoy my accomplishment, someone would come along and top it, or a new and improved version was released immediately after my purchase.

I never really understood the need for competition either, because I've always been confident that I get projects completed. I don't have a problem meeting deadlines. Getting caught up in an urgency to win sucks the satisfaction out of a job well done for me. If I was having an enjoyable moment, working on something and then someone stepped in and encouraged a competition, to crank up the pace and make things "fun"... and then I lose ...so, yay for them! I was bothered that, if I didn't care to compete, why was I always being dragged into competing?

So I stopped it. I dropped all competition. Maybe I didn't start out doing this in the best spirit, but rather than trying to make a bunch of people stop competing with me, I got better results by using self-control and patience along with the other virtues.

If I said, "Guess what?" as a conversation starter, and someone replied with a generic comeback such as "Chicken butt," I stopped talking. It wasn't because I was trying to be "proper," it was because in most cases the topic just wasn't worth the fight. You can say I don't have a sense of humor, but how often must a person laugh at a tired old joke that gets repeated time and again? Maybe I was going to display my humor, but they had interrupted me to take the stage with "chicken butt."

Awkward.

Some conversations were hijacked: I ended up being the listener in my own conversation, which probably isn't a bad exercise in itself. So I went with it and I learned about my control issues while making character studies of others. This process of watching and then learning made me wonder if I really wanted to share anything with some people anyway. Maybe it is best to just let them jabber on while I stay quiet and listen.

For any games, I had to be honest about wanting to participate or not. More often than not, I opted to be a bystander.

I quit trying to make things fair. Life is not fair and it isn't up to me to *make* it fair. It was a huge relief that I didn't owe anyone anything. On the flip side I could drop the score card, because I didn't have to keep tabs on anyone anymore. Once I dropped the competition and gave up the fight for fairness, I noticed that I **can** do things because I want to, and out of the goodness of my heart, not because I think I'm supposed to, or think that I will get anything in return. ***(This is a good thing.)***

Patience is catching all those urges that come up and then waiting to see if there is a better opportunity to indulge, or let them go.

In the end, even though it was tough to drop out of the competition and to learn how to do it without affecting other people, I had learned a lot. Besides, it wasn't permanent. Whenever I feel the push to compete, I have to remember that it's not about me and to just stay the course. All I did was take a step back and use some time to weed out the bad experiences. Now, I can get back to playing a game and look forward to losing. It is all fun and games, after all.

Chapter 5   Conclusion

I had learned some of the biggest life lessons by using a little patience. In itself, patience is the act of shutting up to watch what happens. I learned it wasn't about me. I learned that I control myself and not others. If I want to get things done, I control things and not people. If I think competition sucks, I don't compete. Instead of waiting around to be held accountable for mistakes, I just fix them and move on. And I quit taking on accountability for mistakes that weren't mine.

These lessons were not painful because I kept my little experiment to myself. The result? I wasn't getting wounded by embarrassment, worry and fear. I observed the formula of "new action = new reaction" and got curious to see the outcome.

I didn't pretend to know the results before I went into a situation, because my goal wasn't to prove if I was right or not. I was only curious to see what would happen. I was curious how to achieve love, joy and peace, and I bypassed stewing in embarrassment about something I didn't know.

I found the virtues of patience, faithfulness, and self-control to be the most constraining. My first day with patience seemed to be a lot of holding my breath, clenching my teeth and turning away so I wouldn't get involved. I had to remember to just stay put and that my goal wasn't to avoid things or circumstances. Even though I struggled, I kept going because I was curious. The more curiosity took over, the less restraint I needed. I was absorbing information and naturally redirecting the way I cooperate. It became a case of **when I know better I do better**, which is nice because I don't have to be vigilant to constantly be putting the new me out there.

My work with patience helped me to ease up on the need to be involved in every little thing. I wanted to watch what would happen if I kept my mouth shut and let the other person keep on talking. What would happen if I wasn't the one who got up to help? You know the shield that's always up so you're prepared for anything? What would happen if I let it down? What would happen if I didn't worry about "it," until "it" actually happened; **if** it actually happened? What would happen if I lived in a world where everything was okay and things just moved forward, instead of everything being wrong, then cleaning up the mess with me feeling naughty, naughty, naughty? What would happen if I ended the never ending work to prevent "it" from happening next time?

You can just sit there and guess the answers without doing the work. You can say if **you** don't do it, no one else will. You can say if you let your shield down, you will get wounded. You can ask "why wait?" when you can **prevent** it. So be it. You don't need to waste time to prove that I am wrong. All I am doing is sharing my experiences because I've had some good ones. I now have more good days than bad and that is quite a change.

Epilogue

A funny thing happened on the way to quitting smoking, I found balance in my life. Normally, society will try to tell you not to waste your time and get to quitting, because you will always have problems to face; that's life. Which is true, but if you really can't quit smoking, maybe, just maybe, you might need to get a handle on life before you master the endurance test of withdrawal. Few people take this idea seriously because the need to quit right now is so important. At least that is the way I felt.

My experience was much more valuable to me than to merely go through the process of quitting smoking. People who have read samples of my first manuscript on quitting smoking, told me that my approach wasn't just for smokers. I got hung up on trying to explain anger, worry, and fear, and how they feed the ego, which was making that book too long. I decided to try breaking it into smaller doses. In truth, that is how I came to the process anyway. I stumbled upon something, and I would give it a try, then give it a rest for a couple of days and a little later I would try something else. In small doses, I would sit and ponder on it and then I would go out into the world to watch and learn. If I liked the results, I would keep testing the theory. The key here is that you have to like it. If you don't feel good with the results, don't move forward with it. Wait until you come up with something else.

I felt like I had busted through my arrested development and finally grown up a bit. It is not that I feel old; I still feel young and spry enough to tackle some things that I thought I would never do. Like jogging. My competence is increased without "faking it until I make it." I focused on these virtues and I got good results. It wasn't because I focused on capability and confidence and **how** to get it. I don't ask **how** anymore. Not in the way where I am muddling through life with missing information ... or, without having all my tools.

Now, this in no way means that life is perfect. I always have to fall back on my virtues. And when I don't? That is what forgiveness is for. I don't stand around being sorry or waiting for someone to hold me accountable. I move into recovery, which may include fixing it or letting it go. I don't capture it and hold on to it and fret about it. I move on.

Once I got into doing the process I actually had fun watching the results. It's fascinating. I went in with curiosity, not committed to permanent changes. Don't wait. Start with this one on Patience and just take one day to give it a try. My experience is my experience. Go have your own. What will your experience be?

Acknowledgments

Of course I'd like to thank my family for putting up with me all these years. Thank God he gifted me with you. I'd like to think if I'd had all this stuff down earlier, there would have been at least one less freak-out and maybe I would only have taken up one job instead of two and only held two jobs when I had three.

I'd like to thank Amazon for creating this incredible opportunity. You have reignited the idea that anything is possible in such a tangible way. It is there for us to just reach out and touch it.

I'd like to thank my editor, Dar Streedbeck, I couldn't have made the big crossover to "published" without you. I'd also like to thank my writing group. Not only have you given my spinning wheels traction in edit after edit, but my subject matter stands up when I hold it against our group. When we meet, our writing transcends from being so secret, so personal, and so guarded to being exposed to other people. What's more, it is exposed in a place where the writing is to be scrutinized, ripped apart and threatened. This should be the place where all the bickering, hen pecking and wounded egos happen, but it's not. We explore the creativity of other people's opinions. We thank each other for the corrections so our piece doesn't go out into the greater public with all our flaws. We laugh through the entire meeting, we go home feeling inspired and we can't wait until we meet again. Thank you.